3-D BOOK OF ANGELS

A Collection

by Mary Ruberry

3D Illustrations celestially created by DigiRule Inc.

3-D Revelations Publishing
Newport Beach, CA, USA

3-D Revelations Publishing
537 Newport Center Drive, Suite 282
Newport Beach, CA 92660 USA

ISBN: 0-9641811- 8- 5
Library of Congress Catalog Card Number: 95-61054
Printed in Hong Kong

Book Layout and Cover Design by Joyce Harris
Editing by Norma Collins
Cupid model: Josiah Sandiford

3D Images created by Adelina Banks, Brent Gusdal, Joyce Harris, and Dave Hunter of DigiRule Inc., using computer software and techniques developed and refined by Bohdan Petyhyrycz.

3-D angel viewing instructions on page 32 and back cover.

Experience the magic of all these 3-D books by 3-D Revelations:

3-D Bible Stories
The 3-D Night Before Christmas
*The 3-D Birthday Angel's Party Book
*3-D Magic Bananas and A Bunch of Other Tales in 3-D
* Stereograms for the 3-D Challenged (with 3-D glasses)

*Featuring new patent-pending "Double-Channel 3-D"
Two images in one!
Exclusively from 3-D Revelations

Contents

Snow Angel

"Mortal man is oft controlled
By angel hosts unseen,
Aiding him to here unfold.
More happiness to glean."

Angel Hosts, Edward R. Huxley

Most of us grew up with the innocent glee of making snow angels. We remember lying in the snow, flailing our arms back and forth to achieve the desired angelic form, as giggles arose from our warm breaths. The impression of an angel remains empty in the snow—only its shape tells of the originator.

So it is when pondering angels. The angel imprint leads us to myriad stories and legends surrounding the celestial host. We reflect upon its shape, its nature. We look at footprints, tracking this elusive creature in an effort to gain insight into its habits and habitats.

How intriguing are these beings who stand closest to God. How magical are their movements, how wondrous are their loving ways, how fierce is their will to serve.

Angelic attributes set an idealized standard of noble qualities. Our language contains an abundance of allusions to angelic virtues. If one sings like an angel, one sings sweetly. If one is deemed akin to angels, one is kind and gentle. If one resembles an angel, one is possessed of a sweet expression.

"And further still old legends tell,
The first who breaks the silent spell
To say a soft and pleasing thing,
Hath felt the passing angel's wing!"

The Angel's Wing, Samuel Lover

As we get closer to God's servants in our pursuit, they seem to dance away from vision through the corners of our eyes. But sometimes we can sense them in a quiet moment filled with divine love.

4

Adam and Eve

The Lord God therefore banished him from the garden of Eden, to till the ground from which he had been taken. When he expelled the man, he settled him east of the garden of Eden; and he stationed the cherubim and the fiery revolving sword, to guard the way to the tree of life.

Genesis 3:23,24

Adam and Eve, the first man and woman, experienced an angel encounter. From the beginning, humanity has been inexorably connected with angels, sharing a quest directed by God for divinity... for a return to Paradise.

What is an angel?

The word *angel* comes from a Greek translation of the Hebrew *mal'akh*, meaning 'messenger'. This term describes the primary characteristic of angels in Hebrew and Christian thought. However, many religions throughout history have subscribed to the idea of supernatural messengers or servants of the gods or God.

In John Milton's *Paradise Lost* (written in the middle of the seventeenth century), the Archangel Raphael explains to Adam:

"'Time may come when Men
With Angels may participate, and find
No inconvenient diet, nor too light fare,
And from these corporate nutriments, perhaps,
Your bodies may at last turn all to spirit,
Improved by tract of time, and winged ascend
Ethereal, as we, or may at choice
Here or in heavenly paradises dwell,
If ye be found obedient, and retain
Unalterably firm his love entire
Whose progeny you are'"

Raphael goes on to say:

"Myself, and all the Angelic Host, that stand
In sight of God enthroned, our happy state
Hold, as you yours, while our obedience holds;
On other surety none: freely we serve.
Because we freely love, as is our will
To love or not, in this we stand or fall . . .'"

5

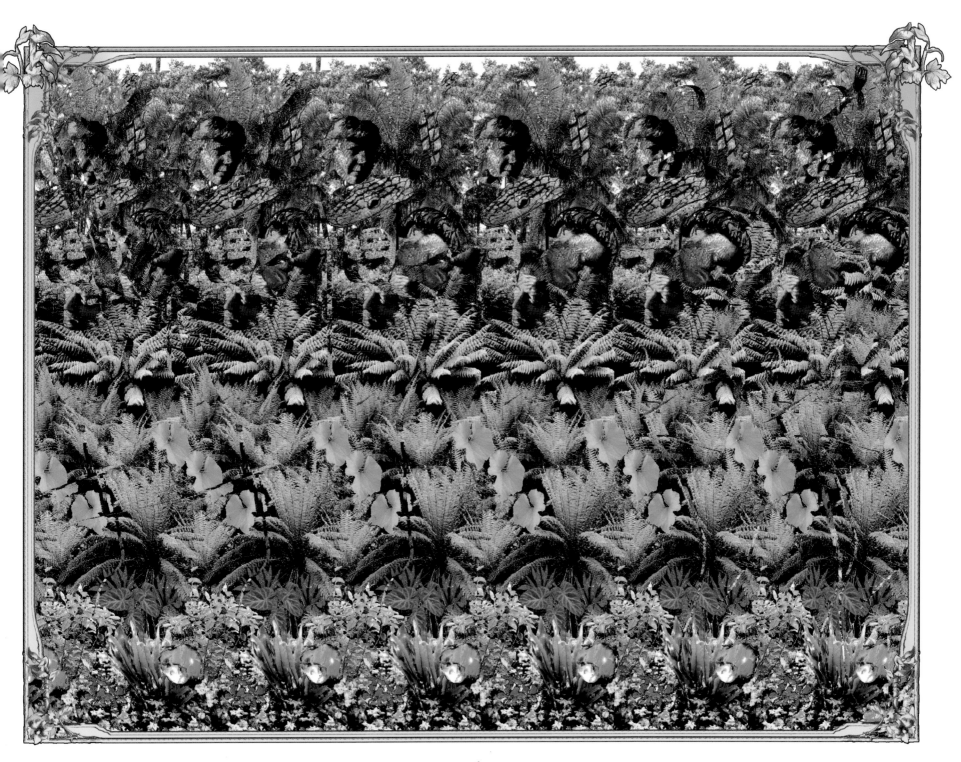

Michael

The most popular angel of all is the Archangel Michael. He is known as the warrior angel and is depicted dressed in full armor, with a sword or staff of justice. His wings are made from peacock feathers, the "eyes" of which symbolize Michael's ability to see into peoples' souls. He is also the "weigher of souls" and as such is often depicted holding scales in his hands, with which he decides who goes to heaven and who goes to hell in the Last Judgment.

Michael holds the position of right-hand angel to God and is considered by most to be the top-ranking angel in the celestial kingdom. Many accomplishments are attributed to Michael, but he is best known for defeating Satan and leading the good angels to victory against the evil forces. Because of this victory, Michael quite often closely resembles the image of St. George as he stands bedecked in shining armor, crushing a dragon-like serpent beneath his feet.

"At that time there shall arise
  Michael, the great prince,
  guardian of your people;
It shall be a time unsurpassed in distress
  since nations began until that time.
At that time your people shall escape
  everyone who is found written in the book.

Many of those who sleep
  in the dust of the earth shall awake;
Some shall live forever,
  others shall be an everlasting horror and disgrace
But the wise shall shine brightly
  like the splendor of the firmament,
And those who lead the many to justice
  shall be like the stars forever."

Daniel 12:1-3

The suffix *el* appearing at the end of angel names means 'radiant' one or 'illumined' and occurs throughout history in successive languages. Therefore, the name Michael is actually Micha-*el*. As we shall see later, the suffix *el* was anglicized to *elf* in Old English, whereby the European fairy traditions sprang.

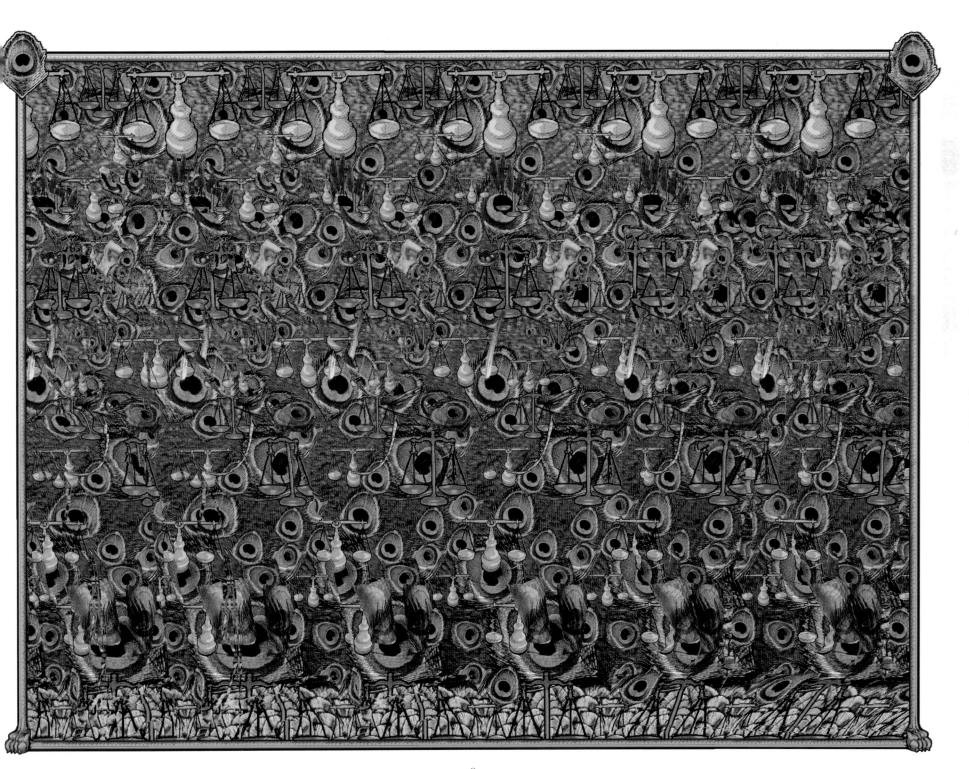

GABRIEL

*In the sixth month, the angel Gabriel was sent from God to a town of
Galilee named Nazareth, to a virgin betrothed to a man named Joseph,
of the house of David. The virgin's name was Mary.*

Luke 1:26,27

General opinion ranks the Archangel Gabriel as the second most popular angel in angel lore. Many consider Gabriel to be the only definitely female angel in the heavenly kingdom. She bears the distinction of being mentioned by name in scriptures more than any other angel, and is said to sit on the left-hand side of the Heavenly Father.

The root of the name, *Gabri*, means governor, power or hero. Gabri-el then means the "governor of Eden" who stands in charge of the Cherubim ranks. According to the Essenes, a brotherhood dating back four thousand years, Gabriel signifies knowledge on their seven-pronged tree of life.

In the old Testament, Daniel reported that the angel Gabriel appeared to him on numerous occasions:

*I was still occupied with this prayer, when Gabriel, the one whom I had seen
before in vision, came to me in rapid flight at the time of the evening sacrifice.*

Daniel 9:21,22

And Joan of Arc claimed that it was the Archangel Gabriel who persuaded her to pursue the Dauphin's cause.

However, the task for which Gabriel gained the greatest fame was that of notifying the Blessed Mother of her pregnancy and subsequent virgin birth. Some speculation exists as to the selection of Gabriel for the job of Mary's visitation. Many consider that Gabriel's distinction as a feminine angel made her the best choice for bringing the impregnation of the Holy Spirit.

*Hail, full of grace, the Lord is with thee. Blessed art thou among women . . . . Do not be afraid, Mary,
for thou has found grace with God. Behold, thou shalt conceive in thy womb and shalt bring forth a son;
and thou shalt call his name Jesus. He shall be great, and shall be called the Son of the Most High.*

Luke 1:28-32

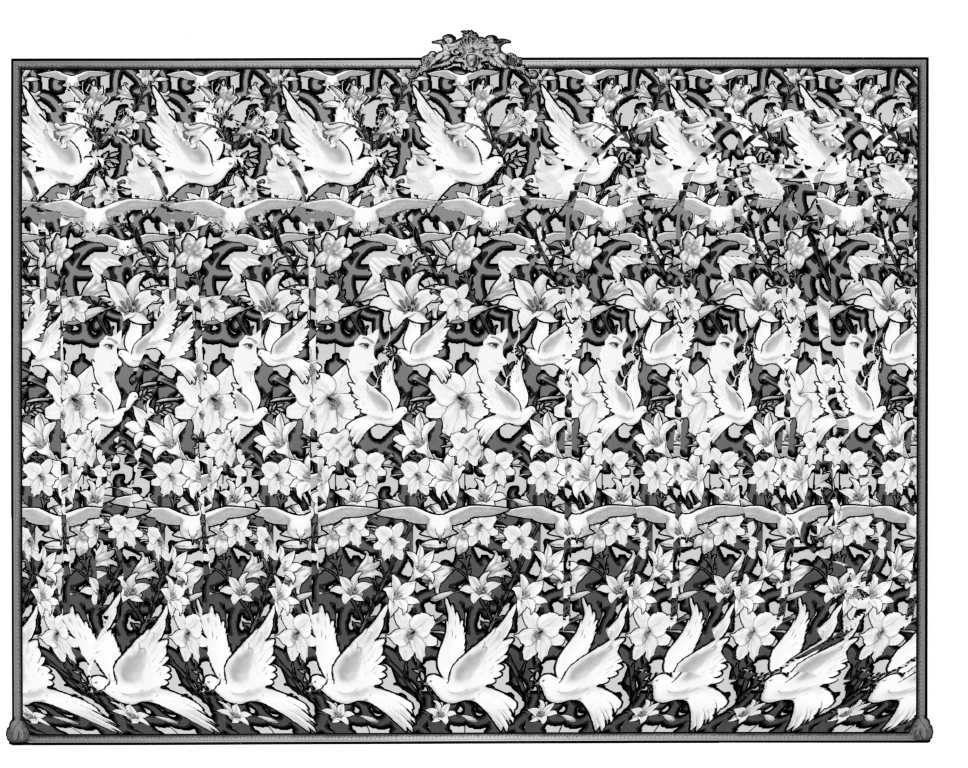

BIRTH OF JESUS

The angel said to them: "You have nothing to fear! I come to proclaim
good news to you - tidings of great joy to be shared by the whole people."
Luke 2:10

When the Savior of the earth was born, it was angels who announced His birth to shepherds who were tending their flocks in the hills outside the town of Bethlehem. These uneducated men and boys were very frightened by the appearance of an angel of the Lord, but the angel told them not to be afraid and then imparted the joyous tidings. The angel told the shepherds that as a sign to them, they could find the Christ child lying in a manger. Then, so the story goes, the sky was suddenly filled with angelic beings, singing God's praises.

Glory to God in high heaven, peace on earth to those on whom his favor rests.
Luke 2:14

The shepherds were so impressed by this display that they hurried into town, found the holy family, and upon viewing the tiny infant, understood what the angels had been telling them. The shepherds then returned to their homes, glorifying and praising God.

The shepherd folk were so moved and excited that they went about telling everyone they met what had come to pass. One can imagine these unassuming fellows walking on clouds after being surrounded by heavenly hosts bestowing joyous tidings.

It came upon the midnight clear,
That glorious song of old,
From angels bending near the earth
To touch their harps of gold
"Peace on the earth, goodwill to men,
From heaven's all-gracious King":
The world in solemn stillness lay
To hear the angels sing.
Edmund H. Sears & Richard S. Willis

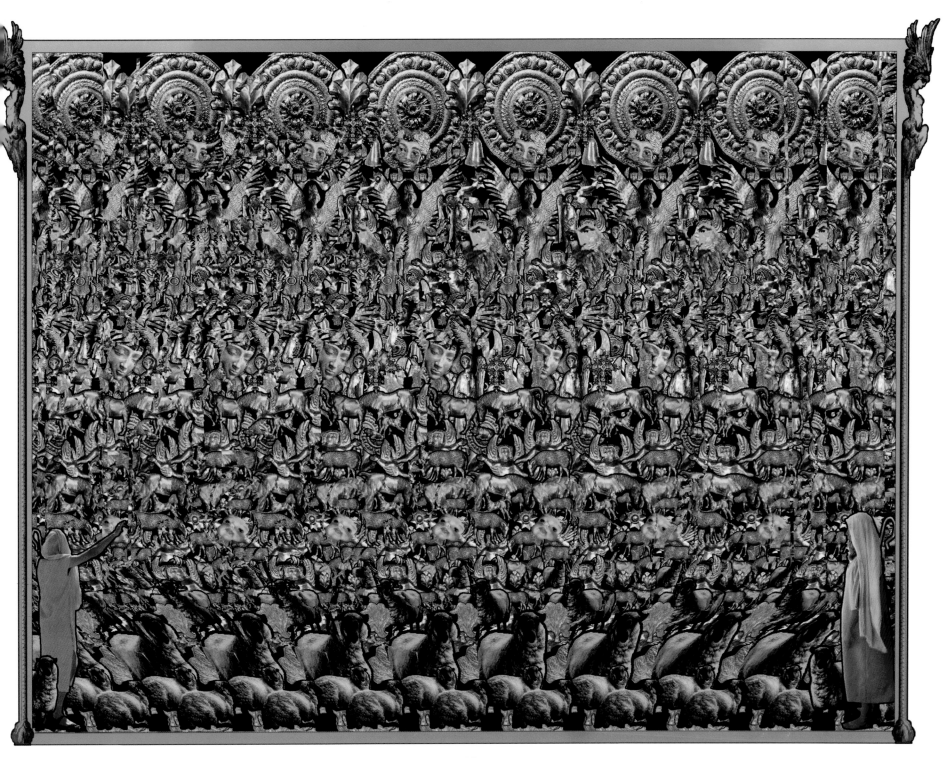

Winged Victory

"Since Victory whose name is glorious has come"

Chorus, *Antigone* by Sophocles

Greek mythology is filled with celestial winged figures. The great king Zeus was constantly sending his gods and goddesses hither and thither to deliver messages or carry out assigned tasks.

Aspects of nature were given divine beings to represent their movements. Daybreak was named Eos, the rosy-fingered dawn with the snowy eyelids. Each day she rose with her wings from the ocean into the sky and dropped the morning dew from a tilted urn.

The moon angel was called Selene (or Mene), sister of Helios, the Sun. The divine Selene of the broad wings began her journey every evening when her brother finished his day and illuminated the night sky with her golden crown.

But undoubtedly the most famous winged figure from ancient Greece is the Hellenistic masterpiece, Winged Victory, also known as the Nike of Samothrace, which dates from 190 B.C.. Nike is sometimes depicted flying through the sky, playing her lute and seducing listeners with her sweet strains.

The lore of Nike can be traced back to the ancient Egyptian goddess of the dead, Nebthet, who was referred to as Nike by Plutarch. According to legend, Nebthet was the sister of Osiris and when he was murdered, she helped her sister Isis embalm his body and mourn her brother with funereal lamentations. Her figure can still be seen decorating sarcophagi and coffin lids as she stretches forth her long, winged arms in protection.

"May Hermes the escorter lead us with his guile, and Athena of the City, who is Victory, always be my protectress."

Odysseus, *Philoctetes* by Sophocles

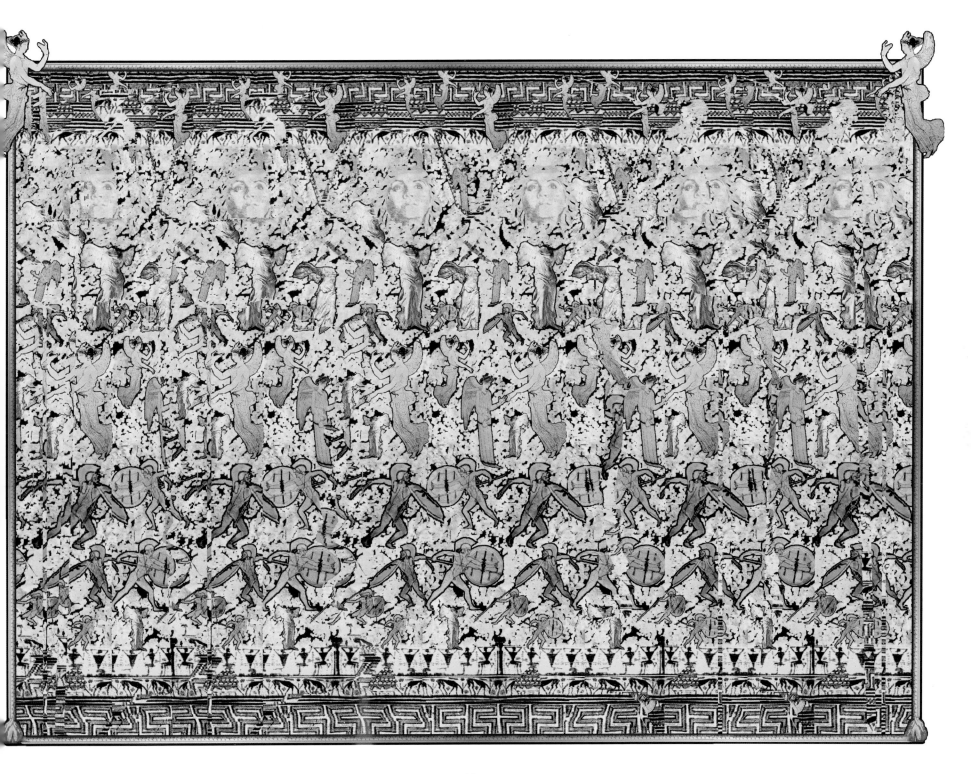

PASSOVER

"He fed the angels cakes of unleavened bread on Passover."

Festival of Passover, Haggadah

How does this night differ from all other nights? Thus begins the child's questions in the traditional Seder dinner of Passover, one of the most important celebrations in the Jewish culture.

Passover memorializes the Israelites' release from oppression and captivity in Egypt when the pharaoh, after considerable persuasion, was finally convinced to let the people go. The final plague that brought about the Israelites' freedom came in the form of an angel. The Angel of Death killed first born children throughout the land, but passed over houses that were marked with blood from a ritually slaughtered animal.

Once again an angel of the Lord is seen as an instrument of God's will, fulfilling a task integral to the divine plan.

Jewish mythology is filled with angel lore. It was an angel of the Lord who stayed the hand of Abraham from killing his son. An angel wrestled with Jacob, thus wounding him in his thigh and bringing about the Jewish practice of abstaining from eating thigh meat of animals. The Book of Daniel contains numerous references to angels, some of whom were reportedly seen by the Babylonian conquerors as well.

About angels, the Talmud (book of teachings) explains:

"From every utterance that issues from the mouth of
the Holy One, blessed be He, an angel is created."

Chagigah 14a

The celebration of Passover remains very meaningful and alive in our contemporary society as the Jewish culture remembers the past, thus rejoicing in the freedoms of the present.

"Mighty in majesty, truly chosen, His angels sing to Him."

Festival of Passover, Haggadah

NATIVE AMERICAN

"To the messengers of the Great Spirit who dwells in the skies above."

Iroquois Constitution

Native Americans of North America refer to angels as helping spirits or guardian spirits. In many tribes, teenage boys go through a vision quest or fast that enables them to meet a helping spirit. When girls reach womanhood, they undergo an isolation through which helping spirits are encountered.

Vision quests are particularly important for shamans who acquire knowledge and also healing skills from their relationships with these helpful angels. The angels give followers information about how to direct energies and work with nature's elements. Only those with a helping (or guardian) spirit were allowed to participate in the *Dream Dance*, *Drum Dance* of the Menominee people.

A common theme in North American legends is a hero character who leaves the world of men and travels to finer realms. There he or she encounters helping spirits who pass on information or enlightenment. In many stories the hero character undergoes a purification ceremony before joining with an angel who bestows guidance.

Helping spirits often take the form of animals, such as Bear or Kind-Old-Man-Buffalo. In the Crow tradition they are called Awakkule, dwarf people. The Creek helping spirits, Yahola and Hayuya, live in the sky and work with health and healing.

In the Innuit tradition, the winged hero called Raven created the world and watches over humanity to offer assistance when difficulties arise. Winged figures are thought to symbolize enlightenment; therefore, feathers are spiritual gifts representing attainment.

"To her and to the child the birds are real people, who live very close the Great Mystery;
the murmuring trees breathe its presence; the falling waters chant its praise."

Ohiyesa, Santee Sioux

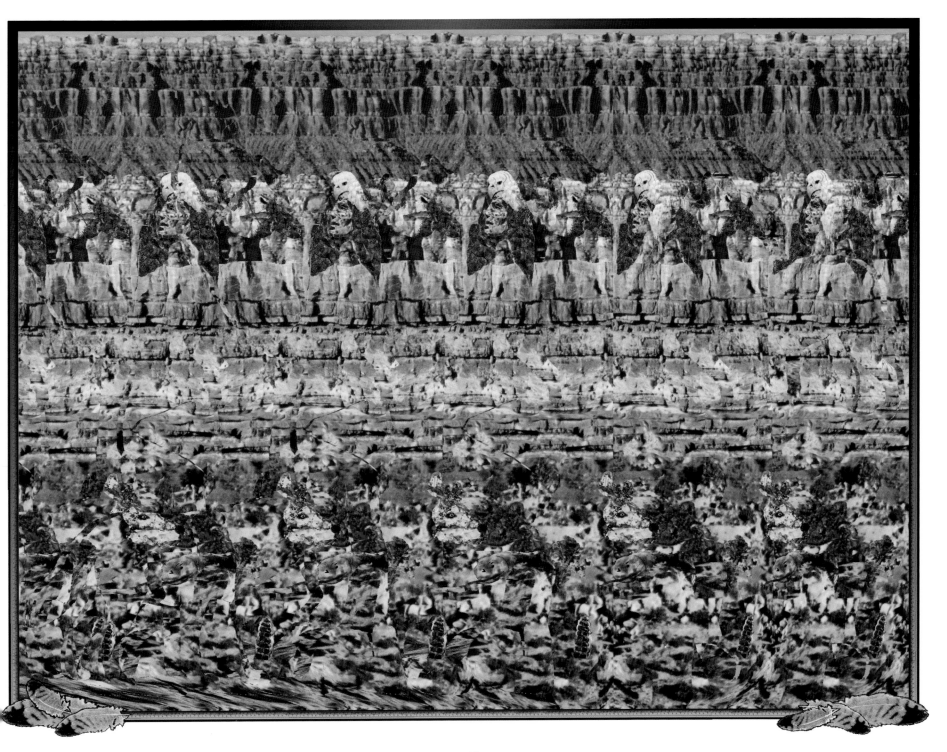

ROMANTIC VERSE

"An angel, robed in spotless white,
Bent down and kissed the sleeping Night.
Night woke to blush; the sprite was gone.
Men saw the blush and called it Dawn."

Dawn, Paul Lawrence Dunbar

The angelic image is softened with Western Europe's romantic perspective. Most famous poets of Western Europe have woven angelic references into the fabric of their verse. Shakespeare, Tennyson, Spenser, Milton, Goethe, Dante, and Browning—to name a few—have all alluded to angels in their famed verbiage.

In particular, the nineteenth-century British artist and poet, William Blake, created many works of art, both visual and written, concerning angels. Following is one of Blake's romantic treatments:

The Angel
by William Blake

I dreamt a dream! What can it mean?
And that I was a maiden Queen
Guarded by an Angel mild
Witless woe was ne'er beguiled!

And I wept both night and day,
And he wiped my tears away;
And I wept both day and night,
And hid from him my heart's delight.

So he took his wings and fled;
Then the morn blushed rosy red
I dried my tears, and armed my fears
With ten thousand shields and spears.

Soon my Angel came again
I was armed, he came in vain;
For the time of youth was fled
And grey hairs were on my head.

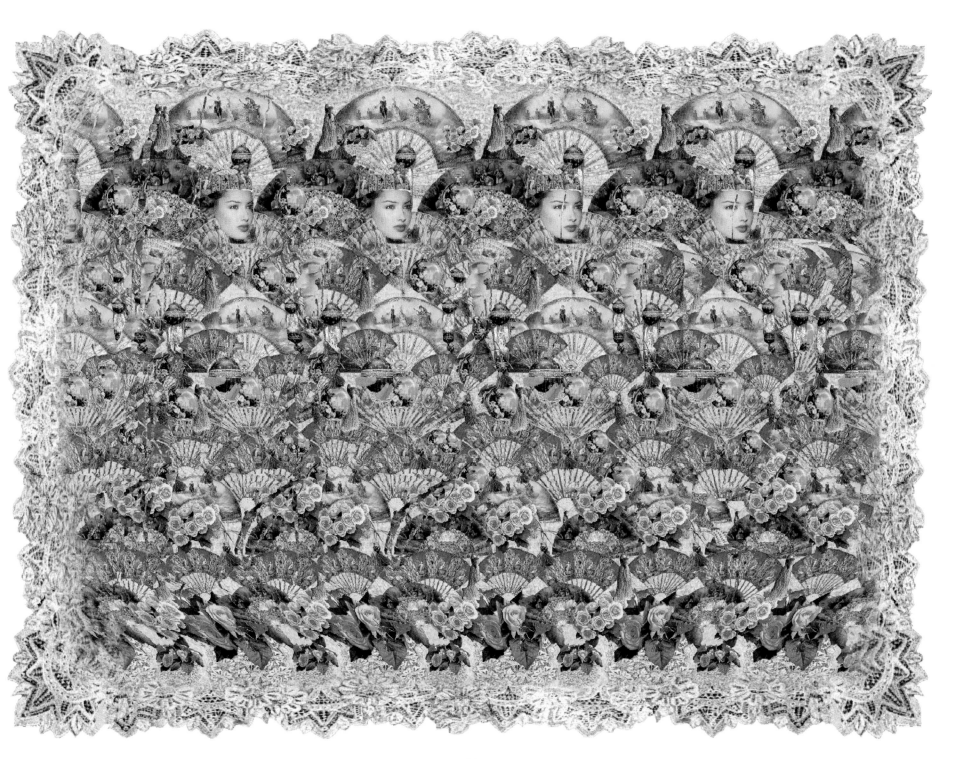

CUPID (EROS)

"Whoever stands up to Eros like a boxer is a fool; for he rules even the gods just as he pleases, and he rules me."

Deianeira, *The Women of Trachis*, Sophocles

The first baby angel is the winged god of love—Eros in the Greek and Cupid in the Roman tradition—and he remains virtually unchanged in aspect since ancient times. Curly hair frames the prankster's face as he enjoys his sport of inflicting love's anguish with the piercing of his arrow.

"Sweet Cupid's shafts, like destiny
Doth causeless good or ill decree.
Desert is born out of his bow,
Reward upon his wing doth go.
What fools are they that have not known
That Love likes no laws but his own!"

Fulke Greville

This playful side of angels was magnified with the introduction of cherubs in the late Middle Ages. Cherubs fill the skies of countless Renaissance paintings and appear as backdrops to both Christian, as well as Pagan themes.

Presently, February 14th provides Cupid with his main opportunities for romantic sport. Named after a Christian martyred in Rome, St. Valentine's Day is widely celebrated by couples declaring their love in 'valentines' that often bear Cupid's image.

"That very time I saw,
Flying between the cold moon and the earth,
Cupid all armed: a certain aim he took
At a fair vestal thronéd by the west,
And loosed his love-shaft smartly from his bow,
As it should pierce a hundred thousand hearts."

William Shakespeare

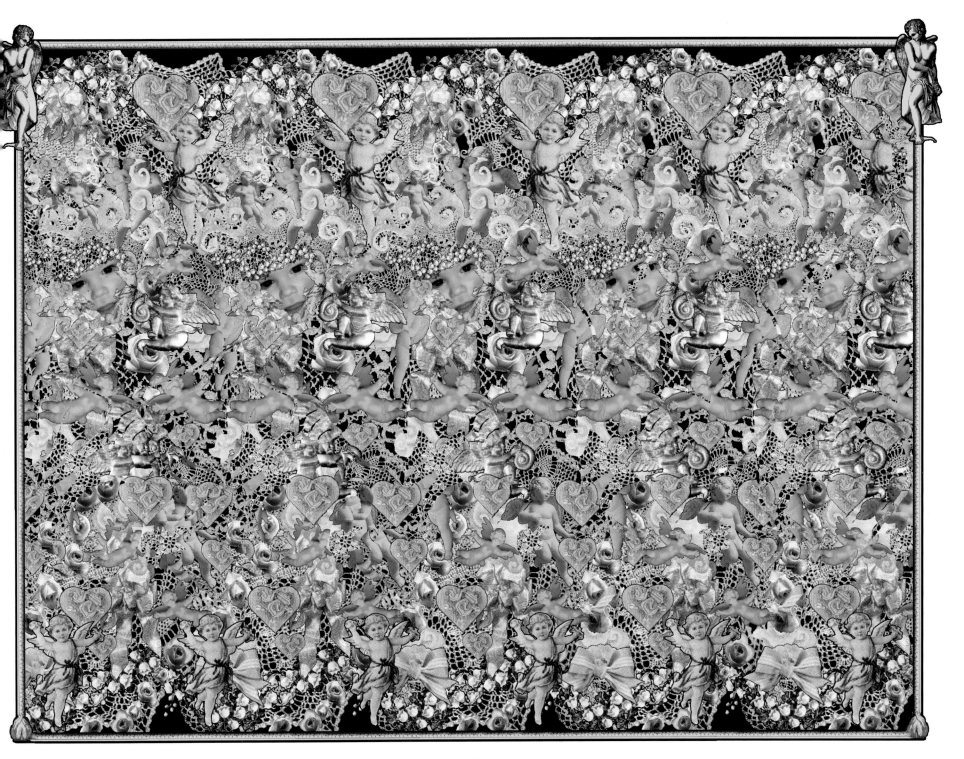

Nature Sprites

"What angel wakes me from my flowery bed?"

A Midsummer-Night's Dream, William Shakespeare

From out of the woods in summer's warmth, a sprightly song of fairies fills the night, their little lanterns bobbing in a merry dance. The angelic suffix *el* (meaning radiant or bright) has been transformed by Old English into *elf*, and thus fairy lore has grown and spread. These are the smallish angels belonging to the realms of nature: tree sprites, flower fairies, angels of the water, angels of the wind.

These wee folk are often depicted as possessing somewhat mischievous dispositions, especially where mortals are concerned. Often we see elves or fairies enjoying usually harmless pranks at the expense of unsuspecting humans.

The most beloved portrayal of these naughty angels is contained in the great masterpiece by William Shakespeare, *A Midsummer-Night's Dream.*

Titania, the Fairy Queen:

"Out of this wood do not desire to go:
Thou shalt remain here, whether thou wilt or no.
I am a spirit of no common rate;
The summer still doth tend upon my state;
And I do love thee: therefore, go with me;
I'll give thee fairies to attend on thee,
And they shall fetch thee jewels from the deep,
And sing while thou on pressed flowers dost sleep:
And I will purge thy mortal grossness so
That thou shalt like an airy spirit go."

Guardian Angels

For to his angels he has given command about you, that they guard you in all your ways.

Psalm 91:11

One of the most enduring and appealing notions of angels is that of guardian. The guardian angel stays by our side, no matter what, sheltering us with unconditional love.

The Talmud states that eleven thousand guardian angels are assigned to each Jewish person at birth. A nineteenth-century children's poem reflects a somewhat diminished number:

"Four angels to my bed, Four angels round my head.
One to watch and one to pray, and two to bear my soul away."

At present, a solitary guardian angel for each soul is commonly accepted.

"Sorrow not my precious children, As you wend life's lonely way.
This may solace: I am with you, Watching o'er you night and day."

The Angel Mother, Edward R. Huxley

For children, the concept of being watched over by one of God's divine servants is particularly strong. The idea of a loving guardian alleviates the fears that commonly besiege little ones. As children, we are comforted by the notion of living under the watchful gaze of someone wiser than ourselves. Upon maturation, our regard either fades or grows more casual as our view of guardian angels develops into what many would describe as companionship or friendship.

"And suddenly my head is covered o'er with those wings, white above the child who prays."

The Guardian Angel, Robert Browning

Perhaps in this one aspect of angels, more than any other, we can see the immensity of God's love for mortal man.

See that you never despise one of these little ones. I assure you,
their angels in heaven constantly behold my heavenly Father's face

Matthew 18:10

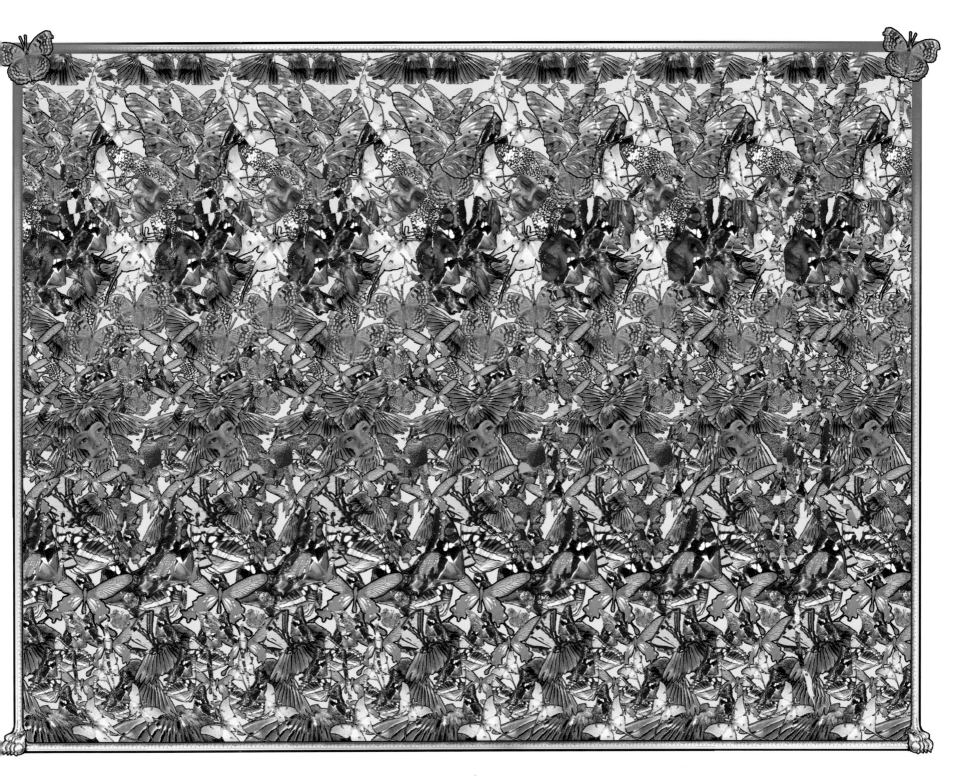

The Three Woes

I heard an eagle flying in midheaven cry out in a loud voice, "Woe, woe, and again woe to the inhabitants of earth from the trumpet blasts the other three angels are about to blow!

Revelation 8:13

St. John the Divine wrote the Book of Revelation during his exile on the Isle of Patmos in 96 A.D. This book describes the apocalyptic end of the world in vivid, colorful, and basically terrifying terms. The main players staging this huge event are the forces of God's angels.

In his dramatic narrative, John describes angels descending from heaven, swooping down to earth, assuming grand and very striking poses and singing in great multitudes. Angels represent the seven churches of God and purge the corrupted earth with their seven pots of plagues, opening of the seven seals, and blowing the thunderous seven trumpets. John refers to the last three trumpets as the Three Woes. Through their scourge, the final cleansing is achieved whereby the Last Judgment begins.

In the Book of Revelation, angels are not dainty creatures. They are mighty, noble, and not at all squeamish as they wipe out one-third of earth's life with one fell blow. We see the wrath of God put into effect unhesitatingly by His angels. They carry out the hellish punishments, then when the seventh trumpet is blown, they sing God's praises throughout heaven.

As death and destruction clear away, however, a message of hope shines through:

There shall be no more death or mourning, crying out or pain, for the former world has passed away.

Revelation 21:4

It is I, John, who heard and saw all these things, and when I heard and saw them I fell down to worship at the feet of the angel who showed them to me. But he said to me: "No, get up! I am merely a fellow servant with you and your brothers the prophets and those who heed the message of this book. Worship God alone!"

Revelation 22:8,9

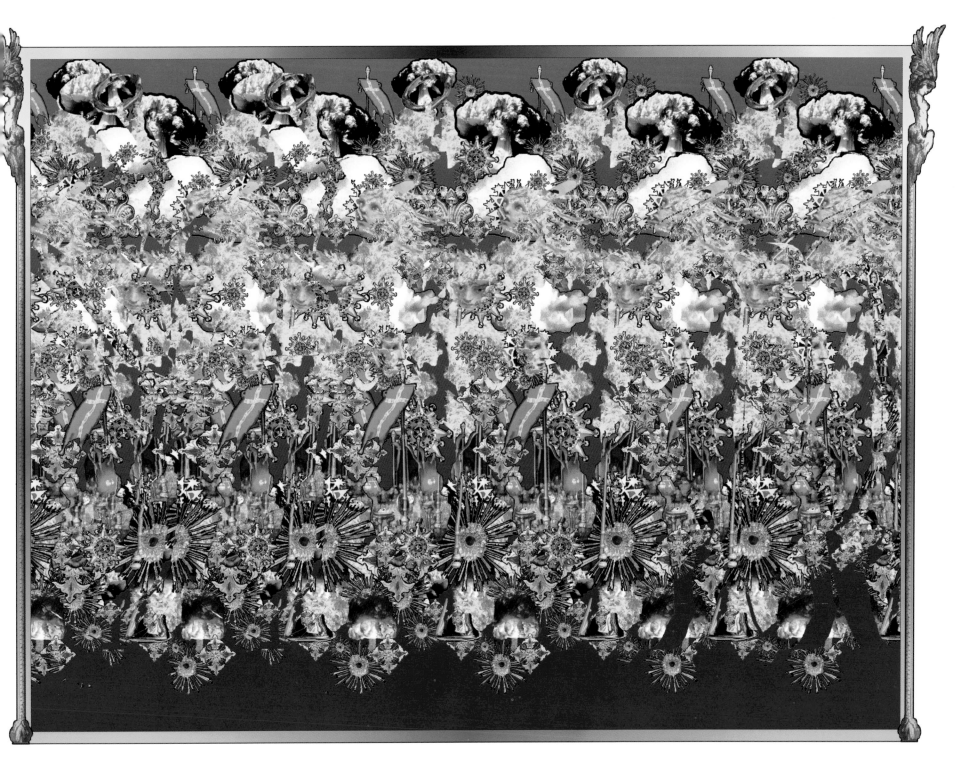

Angel's Whisper

Are they not all ministering spirits, sent to serve those who are to inherit salvation?

Hebrews 1:14

A new relationship with angels is emerging in our time. Close personal relationships and encounters with angels are reported and discussed with ever greater frequency. It seems we are consciously allowing angels to mix closely with us again, as a new movement toward enlightenment grows.

Many people say they can feel an angel's presence—they can sense the comfort and solace emitted by their heavenly companion. Others carry on a dialogue, thus maintaining a personal relationship with an angel being.

Still others claim they work alongside angels, thereby assisting in the efforts to bring the divine plan to fruition. Many individuals have developed insight into nurturing plant life with guidance from angels of nature . . . with spectacular results! There are even artists who paint angels' portraits.

> "I felt an air of wings upon my face,
> Great power moving with majestic grace
> And saw a mighty Angel overhead."

The Angel, Mildred Focht

Numerous reports bear witness to angelic intervention actually saving human lives. Other accounts describe angels directing a person to perform deeds that end up saving someone. Such experiences often renew faith and bring about profound life changes.

Do these angel encounters confirm Milton's masterpiece, whereby our "bodies may at last turn all to spirit" so that "men with angels may participate"?

Do not neglect to show hospitality, for by that means some have entertained angels without knowing it.

Hebrews 13:2

Is there an angel resting on your shoulder? And if you sit very quietly, can you hear an angel whisper?

3-D Solutions

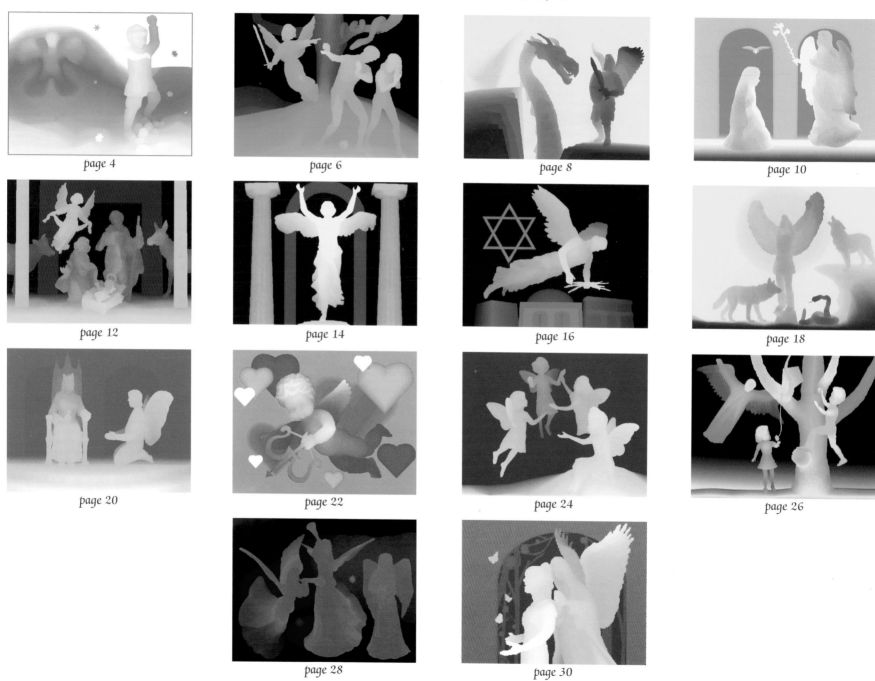

page 4

page 6

page 8

page 10

page 12

page 14

page 16

page 18

page 20

page 22

page 24

page 26

page 28

page 30

3-D Angel Viewing Techniques

3-D angel viewing is a new way to enter into an exciting world of fascination. A rite of passage into 3-D requires you to learn to focus your eyes in a special way. If this is your first time trying to use your 3-D vision, you will need to temporarily suspend the way you've trained your eyes to focus. Some people will see in 3-D almost immediately, while others may struggle a bit. The key is not to get frustrated. Allow yourself to relax and start over as many times as you need to.

There are many ways to trick yourself into 3-D vision. The end result is always the same, you have successfully made your eyes more parallel, or *diverged*. Notice that each 3-D angel work of art is created using a repeating pattern. Diverging your eyes allows you to visually "overlap" the repeating patterns which will give you 3-D vision.

1) Stare at a wall about 8 feet in front of you. Keep your focus on the wall while you raise a 3-D angel illustration 10 inches from your eyes. You will feel as if you are "looking through" the book. Avoid focusing on the surface of the illustration. Instead, allow the page to remain blurry and wait patiently for the 3-D image to appear automatically!

2) Try this method using the front cover artwork. You will notice that there are two faces in a repeating pattern across the page. Focus both eyes on one of the faces in the middle of the page. Slowly bring the illustration toward your face. You will notice that at a closer distance your eyes will no longer be able to hold the focus and the face will appear to split, or double. Now the key is to keep the faces separated and to "overlap" the face onto the next face in the repeating pattern. Once the faces have overlapped you can slowly pull the illustration away to a distance of about 10 inches. Your eyes will now be seeing in 3-D! Again, repeated attempts may be necessary until you can control the overlapping of the faces.

"Good night, sweet prince,
And flights of angels sing thee to thy rest."

Horatio, *Hamlet, Prince of Denmark*, William Shakespeare